Surfing

HE'E NALU

Surfing
HE'E NALU

HAWAIIAN PROVERBS
AND INSPIRATIONAL QUOTES
CELEBRATING HAWAI'I'S ROYAL SPORT

Mutual Publishing

Permission to reprint Hawaiian proverbs and sayings, and
their translations, is courtesy of the Bishop Museum *'Ōlelo
No'eau Hawaiian Proverbs & Poetical Sayings*
by Mary Kawena Pukui (Bishop Museum Press).
Copyright 1983 Bernice Pauahi Bishop Museum.

ISBN 1-56647-637-2

Design by Mardee Domingo Melton

First Printing, November 2003

Mutual Publishing, LLC
1215 Center Street, Suite 210 • Honolulu, Hawai'i 96816
Ph: (808) 732-1709 • Fax: (808) 734-4094
e-mail: mutual@mutualpublishing.com
www.mutualpublishing.com

Printed in Korea

95. Famous Surf Riders. Hawaiian Islands.

Introduction
by U'i Goldsberry

Along Hawai'i's coasts, waves buffet sandy beaches and crash against lava basalt cliffs in fountains of white spray. These rolling breakers may purl against the shoreline as softly as a whisper or pound over the reefs as loudly as a thundering freight train. They reflect the blue of Hawai'i's skies, and glisten in the warmth of the ever-changing Island sun.

For hundreds of years, men and women have played in these waves, bobbing and swimming in the surging tides and steering canoes through towering breakers. But the most dramatic of all of Hawai'i's water amusements is the ancient sport of surfing. Hawaiians described it as *he'e nalu,* or sliding on the waves. To these ancient surfers who rode on rudimentary planks of koa wood, surfing was a metaphor for skill, sex, and displays of courage. Today's athletes use much smaller boards made of foam and fiberglass, equipped with stabilizing fins that ply the water and allow for acrobatic moves that challenge gravity and seem to defy physics. They continue the tradition of bravery and vigor personified in the legends of old.

Surfing: He'e Nalu, a book of celebration filled with proverbs and quotes, honors the men and women who surf the rolling waves of Hawai'i nei. May the great gods of ancient Hawai'i watch over these warriors of the waves, *nā koa o nalu,* these soul surfers who ride the charging blue monsters of the sea.

Inā ʻaʻohe nalu, a laila aku i kai, penei e hea ai:
(If there is no surf, invoke seaward in the following manner:)

Kū mai! Kū mai! Ka nalu nui mai Kahiki mai,
(Arise, arise great surf from Kahiki,)

Alo poʻi pu! Kū mai ka pōhuehue,
(The powerful curling waves. Arise with the pōhuehue.)

Hū! Kai koʻo loa.
(Well up, long raging surf.)

– Ancient Hawaiian chant

…a Sunday afternoon…

The spirit of youth. Boys and girls who
surf are really getting all that Waikiki Beach
has to offer, good fun, good health.

– Tom Blake

Hāʻawi papa heʻe nalu.

A surfboard giving.

To give a thing and later ask for its return.
A surfboard is usually lent, not given outright.

"Far out to the opalescent horizon stretches the ocean in broad bands of jeweled color—turquoise, sapphire, emerald, amethyst; and curving around it like a tawny topaz girdle presses the hard, firm sand of the shore. The pearly surf, diamond crested, sweeps in with a swift, strong surging unlike any sound I have ever heard before; and balanced in superb symmetry on their surfboards, the beach boys come riding toward land."

– Francis Parkinson Keyes

"Waikiki Beach has been kind to me.
The native Hawaiians have been kind.
I have had the honor of riding the big
surfs with these Hawaiians—watched their
most beautiful women dance the hulas—
I have been invited into their exclusive
Hui Nalu surfriding club—a club for
natives only. I have held the honor
position (bow seat) riding waves in
the outrigger canoe—the honor position
(holding down the outrigger) on the sailing
canoe. I have been initiated into the secrets
of spearfishing far out on the coral reefs.
I have learned much from these people."

– Tom Blake

"Never turn your back on the ocean."

– Hawaiian saying

**O ka papa he'e nalu kēia,
pahe'e i ka nalu ha'i o Makaiwa.**

This is the surfboard that will glide in the rolling surf of Makaiwa.

A woman's boast. Her beautiful body is like the surfboard
on which her mate "glides over the rolling surf."

...silvery waves...

An unbelievable sense
of accomplishment goes
with a successful ride.

– Tom Blake

"Surfing big waves is all about overcoming fear. Fear paralyzes and fear causes hesitation, and fear is something that we all have…. So every year, if you're going to surf big waves, you have to go through a process of mentally and physically preparing yourself. The physical part is relatively simple–you have to be fit, you swim, you run. But the mental part is a lot more challenging because you have to revisit those old fears and you have to overcome them."

– Jim Howe

E ho'i ka u'i o Mānoa, ua ahiahi.

Let the youth of Mānoa go home, for it is evening.

Refers to the youth of Mānoa who used to ride the surf at Kalehuawehe in Waikīkkī. The surfboards were shared among several people who would take turns using them. Those who finished first often suggested going home early, even though it might not be evening, to avoid carrying the boards to the *hālau* where they were stored. Later the expression was used for anyone who went off to avoid work.

"Surfing is very much like making love.
It always feels good—no matter how many
times you've done it. But what is most
important about surfing—as with loving—
is its worth to the individual. There's
a strong sense of fulfillment—
as opposed to frustration."

– Paul Strauch

Hāwāwā ka heʻe nalu haki ka papa.

When the surf rider is unskilled, the board is broken.

An unskilled worker bungles instead of being a help.
There is also a sexual connotation:
When the man is unskilled, the woman is dissatisfied.

"I think we have to teach a lot of these kids to first be gentlemen…Try to help one another and not hog the doggone waves. You know, there are so many waves coming in all the time, you don't have to worry about that. Just take your time—wave comes. Let the other guys go; catch another one. And that's what we used to do. We'd see some other fella there first, and we'd say, 'You're here first. You take the first wave.'"

– Duke Kahanamoku

Duke Kahanamoku
Hawaiian Swimmer

DUKE

"The boards the kids are using today are okay but they're too light for me. My board was 16 feet of California redwood. I made it myself at Waikiki without calipers to shape it. I would just feel it and say, need a little off here, that's pretty good, little bit here, and so on, until it was like I wanted it."

– Duke Kahanamoku

"And one sits and listens
to the perpetual roar, and watches
the unending procession, and feels
tiny and fragile before this tremendous
force expressing itself in fury and foam
and sound. Indeed, one feels microscopically
small, and the thought that one may wrestle
with this sea raises in one's imagination a
thrill of apprehension, almost of fear."

– Jack London

"Surfing is an individual expression of one's own worth and one's own ability to participate directly with nature. And what makes it really enjoyable to me is that every wave is different… there's a special, non-repetitive pleasure in it that never gets boring."

– Otis Chandler

**Hō aʻe ka ʻike heʻe nalu
i ka hokua o ka ʻale.**

Show [your] knowledge of surfing
on the back of the wave.

Talking about one's knowledge and
skill is not enough; let it be proven.

"I can remember looking up at this 25-foot wave, and time stopped. It was like a still photograph. I was one with the wave, I was one with the water, with my surfboard, my body. The entire universe just melted together for that one second."

– Fred Van Dyke

**He ʻo ʻia ka mea
hāwāwā e ka heʻe nalu.**

The unskilled surf rider falls back into the water.

"A glistening Polynesian youth
gliding gracefully on a surfboard has
become a symbol of all the tropical pleaures
Hawai'i has to offer the careworn Westerner.
With Diamond Head as a backdrop, the
beachboy guiding a canoe-load of laughing
malihini (newcomers) down the slope of a
wave at Waikiki has become the world's
image of 'The Paradise of the Pacific.'"

– Ben Finney and James D. Houston

La'i lua ke kai.

The sea is very calm.

All is peaceful.

He kāʻeʻaʻeʻa pulu ʻole no ka heʻe nalu.

An expert on the surfboard who does not get wet.

Praise of an outstanding surfer.

Kai nuʻu a Kāne.

Kāne's rising sea.

The foamy sea that follows after a tumbling wave.

"My family believes we came from the ocean. And that's where we're going back."

– Duke Kahanamoku

MID-PACIFIC
CARNIVAL
FEB. 18 to 21
1914
DUKE KAHANAMOKU
CHAMPION SWIMMER OF THE WORLD
HONOLULU HAWAII

"Lōkahi is mind, body and soul. To just strengthen your physical self is not enough. To strengthen yourself mentally is not enough. To strengthen yourself spiritually is not enough. To strengthen yourself physically, mentally and spiritually is Lōkahi."

– Brian Keaulana

"It's indescribable—the rush and the whole adrenalin thing. When you're done, you feel like you conquered something so big and so insane. There's nothing like it, for sure."

– Sierra Emory

"In the early times the art of surfing had
a profound religious significance; it was called
Ka Nalu, a study of the wave. From a lifetime
in and around the ocean, a surf rider learned
some of the immutable laws of nature. From
the many hundreds of hours spent off shore
on his surfboard, he became aware of a constant
pattern that prevails in the forming and breaking
action of the waves. Thus, he came to recognize
the great harmony and rhythm that permeates
all things. He acquired the patience to wait
for things to happen rather than to try to
make them happen. With each successful ride,
he experienced a feeling of spiritual achievement;
he came into harmony with nature; and nature,
for all practical purposes, is God.

– Tom Blake

These Hawaiian beachboys
seemed to weave a spell of the real
Hawai'i over the assemblage. Tourists and
local residents alike sat quietly while they
listened, enchanted, to the island music that
stirred the heart…The boys had no set
program, for it was all informal, but they
would play and sing song after song,
a surf of melody.

– Johnny Noble, composer *Waikiki Beachboy*

"Men of the sun and sea
Those men who ride mountains
Bend to the wind
Top to bottom, side to side
Looking for the ultimate ride"

– Israel Kamakawiwo'ole

"Just get away from the shady turf,
And baby catch some rays on the sunny surf.
And when you catch a wave,
You'll be sitting on top of the world."

– Brian Wilson (The Beach Boys)

References

Blackburn, Mark. *Surf's Up: Collecting the Longboard Era.* Pennsylvania: Schiffer Publishing Ltd., 2001.

Blake, Tom. *Hawaiian Surfriders, 1935.* California: Mountain & Sea Publishing, 1983.

Brennan, Joseph L. *Duke: The Life Story of Hawai'i's Duke Kahanamoku.* Honolulu: Ku Pa'a Publishing Incorporated, 1994.

Coleman, Stuart Holmes. *Eddie Would Go: The Story of Eddie Aikau, Hawaiian Hero.* Honolulu: MindRaising Press, 2001.

Finney, Ben, and Houston, James D. *Surfing: A History of the Ancient Hawaiian Sport.* California: Pomegranate Artbooks, 1996.

Hall, Sandra and Ambrose, Greg. *Memories of Duke.* Honolulu: Bess Press, 1995.

Lueras, Leonard. *Surfing: The Ultimate Pleasure.* Honolulu: Emphasis International Ltd., 1984.

Lyon, Charlie and Leslie, and Max, Blue. *Jaws Maui.* Waialua: Jaws Maui Ltd., 1997.

Pukui, Mary Kawena. *'Ōlelo No'eau: Hawaiian Proverbs and Poetical Sayings.* Honolulu: Bishop Museum Special Publication No. 71, 1983.

Timmons, Grady. *Waikiki Beachboy.* Honolulu: Editions Limited, 1989.

Van Dyke, Fred. *Surfing Huge Waves with Ease.* Honolulu: Mutual Publishing, 1992.

Photo Credits